O Christmas Tree, O Christmas Tree, How lovely are your branches!

This Christmas season your tree can sparkle as never before when you make all of the dazzling ornaments in this book. Some of the materials you need to make your ornaments are included here. In the materials list they will appear in italic print. You will also need some easy-to-find craft supplies.

Before you begin working on an ornament, read through the directions and gather all the materials. You will have to use patterns to make many of the ornaments in this book. Here is how to transfer a pattern.

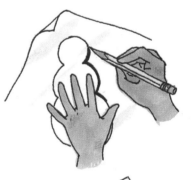

You will need:

tracing paper
soft-leaded pencil
scissors

1. Place the tracing paper over the ornament pattern in the book. Trace the pattern onto the tracing paper.

2. With the soft-leaded pencil, darken the lines of the pattern.

3. Place the tracing paper—pencil side down—on the paper or fabric you need for the ornament. With the pencil, go over the darkened lines. Remove the tracing paper and cut out the shape.

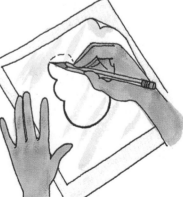

NORTHERN LIGHTS BEAR

You will need:

★ glue

★ 8" x 3" (20 cm x 7.5 cm) piece of silver metallic paper or foil

★ 4" x 3" (10 cm x 7.5 cm) rectangle of lightweight cardboard

★ tracing paper

★ pencil

★ scissors

★ 4" (10 cm) length of red or green ribbon, ¼" (.6 cm) or ½" (1.25 cm) wide

★ 2 or 3 beads

★ *7" (17.5 cm) length of red or gold ribbon, 1/8" (.3 cm) wide* (or cord or colored string)

★ 2" x 2" (5 cm x 5 cm) square of green construction or gift paper

★ 6" (15 cm) length of silver cord or thread

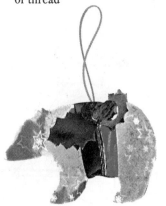

This bear will bring plenty of polar sparkle to your tree!

1. Glue the silver metallic paper to both sides of the lightweight cardboard. Transfer the bear pattern to the silver covered cardboard. (See page 1 for instructions on how to transfer a pattern.) Carefully cut out the bear shape.

2. Decide which side will be the back of your bear. Starting from the back, wrap the red or green ribbon tightly around the middle of the bear. Overlap the ends of the ribbon and glue them together at the back.

3. To decorate the bear, string the beads on the ⅛" (.3 cm) thick ribbon. Tie the ribbon and beads around the bear's middle. Cut off the excess ribbon.

4. Transfer the holly leaf pattern to the green paper. Make 2 or 3 leaves and cut them out. Glue one end of each leaf under the beads.

5. To make a hanging loop, slide the silver cord under the narrow ribbon on the bear's back. Tie the ends of the cord in a knot and hang your bear on the tree.

Besides hanging this cheerful ornament on the tree, you can also tie it to a special present. Or add a safety pin to the back and wear it on your coat when you go caroling.

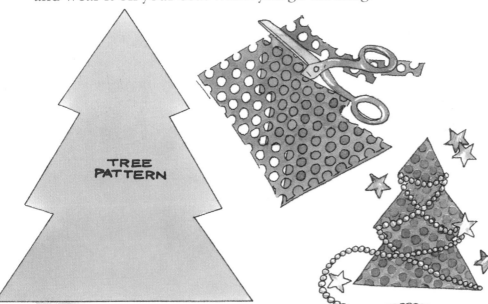

TREE PATTERN

1. Transfer the tree pattern to the green construction paper. (See page 1.) Cut out the tree shape.

2. Glue the punched metallic ribbon to both sides of the tree. Following the shape of the tree, carefully cut away the excess ribbon.

3. Decorate the tree starting with the gold-bead chain. Drape the beads across the tree, securing each corner with glue. Glue stars on the tips of the branches and one star to the top of the tree.

4. Attach thread to the top of the tree to hang your ornament.

SURPRISE PACKAGE

You will need:

★ 2 ¾" x 3" (7 cm x 7.5 cm) rectangle of white cardboard
★ ruler
★ scissors
★ 6" x 4" (15 cm x 10 cm) piece of gold lace
★ 12" (31 cm) length of gold paper twist
★ 2" x 2" (5 cm x 5 cm) square of red construction or gift paper
★ 5" (12.5 cm) length of red ribbon, ⅛" (.3 cm) wide
★ glue
★ white or gold thread
★ ½ gold tinsel pipe cleaner
★ gold cord

You can personalize this ornament by writing the name of a special friend on the gift tag. Or make several packages in various colors and sizes and hang them on your tree.

1. Wrap the gold lace around both sides of the rectangle. Cut excess fabric away from the edges and glue down the fabric edges.

2. Unwind the gold paper twist and cut 3 narrow strips about ⅛" (.6 cm) wide from the full length of the paper.

3. From the remaining gold paper, cut a piece 3" (7.5 cm) long. Twist it in the center to make a bow. Secure the bow with thread and knot it, leaving a 2" (5 cm) tail on each end of the thread. Tie a bow with the red satin ribbon and attach it to the gold bow with the loose thread.

4. Wrap each narrow strip of gold paper lengthwise around the package and tie at the top with a knot. Tie the 3 strips to one another at the top with thread and clip off the ends. Add the gold and red bow to the package using the ends of the thread to secure it in place.

5. Make a tiny gift tag from the red construction or gift paper and attach it to the package. Attach a gold tinsel pipe cleaner and gold cord hanger.

CHRISTMAS ELF GARLAND

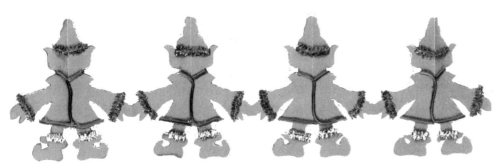

You will need:

★ sheet of gift or plain light-weight green paper
★ ruler
★ pencil
★ scissors
★ tracing paper
★ glue

Optional: *silver or gold tinsel pipe cleaner, red or gold cord*

Christmas is on its way. Make this elf garland to welcome Santa to your home.

1. Cut a strip of paper 12" (30 cm) long x 4" (10 cm) wide.

2. Transfer the pattern of the elf onto one end of the paper. (See page 1.) Make sure that the elf's hand is on the edge of the paper.

3. Keep the elf outline on top and fold the paper accordion style, as shown. Make 7 even folds, being careful that the top and bottom edges of the paper line up with each other.

4. Carefully cut out the elf shape. Make sure you cut through all 8 layers of paper. Unfold the paper and you'll have a garland of 4 elves. Make as many sets of elves as you would like and glue them together to form a longer garland.

5. Decorate the elves, if you'd like. Try gluing small pieces of silver or gold tinsel pipe cleaner to their hats, wrists, and boots. Add red or gold cord to trim their jackets. Then hang the elves on the tree or over a door frame. You can even use strings of elves as streamers at a party.

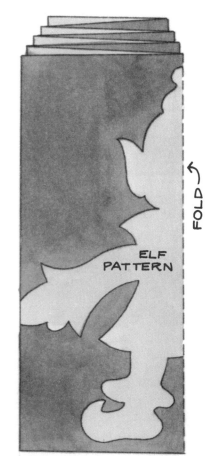

FOLD

ELF PATTERN

RED-NOSED REINDEER

You will need:

★ 9" x 9" (22.5 cm x 22.5 cm) square of blue construction paper
★ pencil
★ tracing paper
★ scissors
★ black marker or pen
★ small scraps of silver paper or foil
★ glue or glue stick
★ 5" (12.5 cm) length of red ribbon, ⅛" (.3 cm) wide
★ silver tinsel pipe cleaner
★ silver thread

This reindeer's shiny nose will help Santa find his way to your tree!

1. Fold the construction paper in half. Transfer the reindeer pattern and the ear pattern onto the construction paper. (See page 1.) The reindeer's back should line up with the fold in the construction paper. Cut out the reindeer's body. Cut out two ears.

2. Fold the reindeer's tail as shown. To make the reindeer's neck, fold the paper to the left. Then fold the neck again, this time to the right to make the head. Make the last fold to the left to form the nose. Keep your folds sharp.

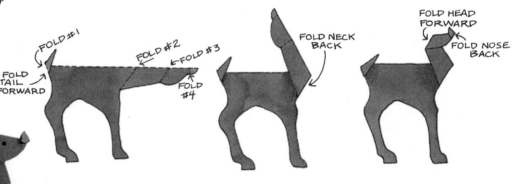

3. Unfold the neck creases and the tail and open up the reindeer's body. Pull the tail up so it folds and makes an upside down V. Pull the neck back at the bottom crease. Fold the neck forward at the second crease and back at the third crease.

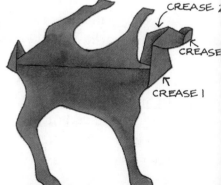

6

4. Cut a small half-circle of red ribbon for the nose. Glue it in place. Then fold the reindeer in half again along its back. Make dots with a pencil where you think the reindeer's eyes should be and color the spots in with the black marker.

5. Cut out small pieces of silver paper for the feet and glue them to the reindeer. (HINT: retrace the feet from the pattern to help you get the right size and shape.) For the spots, cut out some little silver paper circles and glue them to the reindeer.

6. Fold the pipe cleaner in half. Bend it into antlers with three loops on each half. Place the antlers in the 'v' at the back of the head and glue them in place. Glue on the ears.

7. Loop the length of red ribbon around the reindeer's neck and glue the ends together to form reins. Attach a loop of silver thread to the reindeer's back and hang him on your tree.

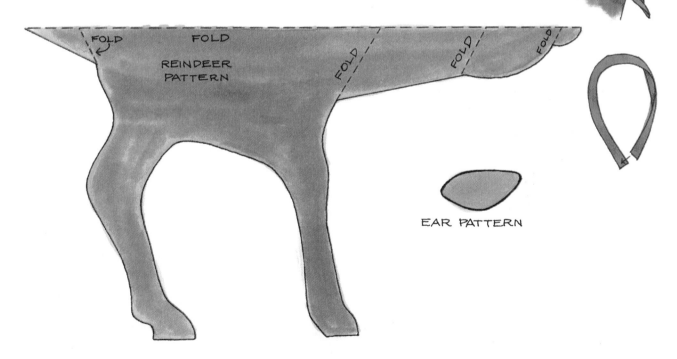

FOLD FOLD

REINDEER PATTERN

FOLD FOLD FOLD

EAR PATTERN

WOODEN SOLDIER

You will need:

★ *wooden clothespin*
★ black marker
★ 5" x 5" (12.5 cm x 12.5 cm) square of blue construction or gift paper
★ scissors
★ glue
★ *12" (31 cm) length of red ribbon, ⅛" (.3 cm) wide*
★ 4" x 4" (10 cm x 10 cm) square of silver foil or gift paper
★ 3" x 3" (7.5 cm x 7.5 cm) square of white construction paper
★ *2 metallic stars*
★ 3 ½" (9 cm) length of red paper ribbon, ¼" (.6 cm) wide
★ gold thread
★ 3" (7.5 cm) length of silver cord

Make a battalion of these soldiers to guard the presents under your tree.

1. Use the black marker to paint shoes on each "leg" of the clothespin.

2. To make the pants, cut 2 pieces of blue paper 2" x 2" (5 cm x 5 cm). Wrap each "leg" with blue paper. Begin by drawing the paper through the clothespin, then bring the edges together along the side of the leg and glue in place.

3. Cut 2 pieces of red ribbon 2¼" (6 cm) long. With a small amount of glue, attach the red ribbon along the outer seam of each pant leg.

4. Cut a 1" x 2½" (2.5 cm x 6 cm) piece of silver foil. Wrap the soldier's body with foil. Fold the extra foil under and glue in place. Shape the shoulders and neck by pressing the foil against the clothespin.

5. Cut a 6" (15 cm) piece of red ribbon. Wrap the ribbon around the soldier's body, as shown. Start with the center of the ribbon at the back of the neck. Wrap the ends around the front and make an X with the ribbon across the soldier's chest. Glue in place with the ends of the ribbon at the back.

6. For the belt, cut a piece of silver cord long enough to go around the soldier's waist. Glue the cord in place.

8

7. Following the patterns below, cut out a right arm and a left arm from white construction paper. (See page 1.) Leaving the hands white, cover the sleeves with silver foil. Note which arm is the right and which is the left.

8. Decorate the soldier's sleeves. Cut strips from the blue construction paper and glue them on the sleeves. Glue small pieces of red ribbon at the cuffs. Add a red star to both sleeves. When all the glue is dry, glue each arm to the correct side of the clothespin.

9. To make the hat, cut a 2¼" x 1" (6 cm x 2.5 cm) piece of blue paper. Snugly roll the paper around the head of the clothespin. Glue the ends of the paper together.

10. To make the silver plume, cut a piece of silver paper 2" x ¾" (5 cm x 1.9 cm). Fold the paper accordion style with the folds about ⅛" (.3 cm) apart. Spread the folds into a fan shape and tie the base of the plume with gold thread. Glue the plume to the front of the hat.

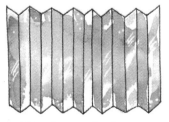

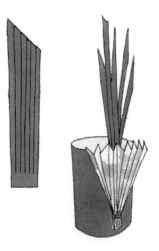

11. To make the red plume, cut 2 pieces of red paper ribbon 1¾" (4.5 cm) long. Cut one end of the ribbon into narrow strips and glue it inside the hat crown.

12. Tie some silver cord or thread around the soldier's neck. Now hang your ornament from the tree!

BALLERINA GIRL

You will need:

★ white, red, black, brown, and yellow tempera paints
★ *wooden clothespin*
★ small paintbrush
★ colored markers
★ tracing paper
★ pencil
★ glue
★ scissors
★ *silver tinsel pipe cleaner*
★ 20" (50 cm) length of red metallic ribbon, ¼" (.6 cm) wide
★ 6" x 10" (15 cm x 25 cm) sheet of metallic cellophane or tissue paper
★ stapler
★ 2 cotton balls
★ *gold-bead string*
★ gold cord

Invite this pretty ballerina to dance on the branches of your tree!

1. Mix the tempera paints to match your flesh tone. Paint the clothespin. Let the paint dry.

2. After the paint has dried, paint the shoes pink. (Mix red and white paint to make pink.) Draw in the ballerina's face with paint or with a marker. Practice drawing the face on scrap paper first. Color in the hair, too. Allow the paint to dry.

3. To make the arms, cut the silver tinsel pipe cleaner in half. Fold each one in half and twist to double its thickness. Glue each pipe cleaner to the ballerina's sides so that the arms reach above her head.

4. To complete the ballerina's shoes, cut a 6" (15 cm) piece of red metallic ribbon. Carefully cut the ribbon in half lengthwise. Start with one end of the ribbon on the inside of the ballerina's leg ½" above the shoe. Wrap the ribbon in a crisscross pattern above the shoe, as shown.

5. Stretch out the cotton balls a little and wrap them around the ballerina's body. Glue them in place.

10

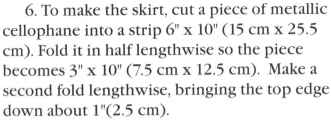

6. To make the skirt, cut a piece of metallic cellophane into a strip 6" x 10" (15 cm x 25.5 cm). Fold it in half lengthwise so the piece becomes 3" x 10" (7.5 cm x 12.5 cm). Make a second fold lengthwise, bringing the top edge down about 1"(2.5 cm).

7. Place the remaining 14" (36 cm) of red metallic ribbon inside the fold. Make sure that the ribbon is snug against the inside of the fold. Carefully staple the cellophane together just below the ribbon in 6 or 8 places. Make sure you do not catch the ribbon in the staples.

8. Hold the ribbon on both sides of the cellophane. To form the gathers of the skirt, gently scrunch the cellophane together along the ribbon.

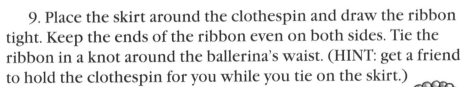

9. Place the skirt around the clothespin and draw the ribbon tight. Keep the ends of the ribbon even on both sides. Tie the ribbon in a knot around the ballerina's waist. (HINT: get a friend to hold the clothespin for you while you tie on the skirt.)

10. To make a double crown, wrap one end of the gold-bead string around the ballerina's head twice. Cut off the extra string and glue the crown in place.

11. To make a hanger, glue a loop of gold cord on top of the ballerina's head.

11

SINGING ANGEL

You will need:

- ★ gold metallic lace
- ★ scissors
- ★ sheet of white tissue paper or face tissue
- ★ white thread
- ★ 5" (12.5 cm) length of gold paper twist
- ★ 10" (25 cm) length of gold cord
- ★ Styrofoam ball
- ★ gold tinsel pipe cleaner
- ★ glue
- ★ 2 ½" (6 cm) length of gold-bead chain
- ★ small piece of blue construction paper
- ★ 1 metallic star
- ★ needle with a large eye
- ★ 6" (15 cm) length of gold thread or cord

This pretty angel will sing about the joys of Christmas.

1. Cut the gold lace to 5" x 6" (12.5 cm x 15 cm). Fold the tissue paper in half and cut a double layer to the same size.

2. Place the tissue paper on top of the lace and fold the two pieces in half with the tissue on the inside. To form the skirt, pinch and gather the cut edges together. Wrap the gathered edge with thread and secure with a double knot. Then wrap all 10" (25 cm) of the gold cord around the top of the gathered skirt to make the angel's body.

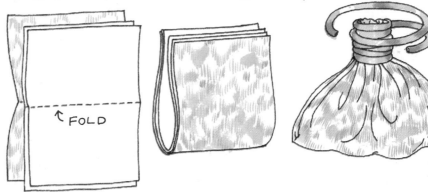

3. To make the hanger, thread the needle with the gold thread. Double knot the ends together. Carefully run the needle up through the center of the Styrofoam ball. Cut the thread next to the needle and knot the two ends. To make the head, glue the Styrofoam ball on top of the angel's body.

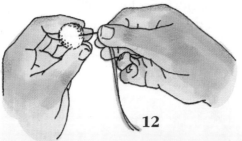

12

4. To make a crown, cut the pipe cleaner in half. Using one piece, form a small circle and twist the ends around one another to hold the shape. Glue the crown to the angel's head. For the halo, make a circle from the gold-bead chain and glue it to the back of the angel's head.

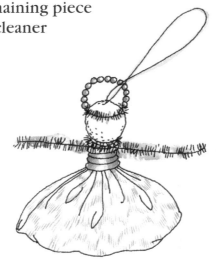

5. Make the arms with the remaining piece of pipe cleaner. Center the pipe cleaner on the back of the angel's neck. Wrap the arms around and cross them in front.

6. To form the wings, unwind and flatten the gold paper twist. Gather the gold paper in the center to make a bow shape. Secure the bow by wrapping thread around the center. Tie a double knot. Glue the gold wings to the back of the angel.

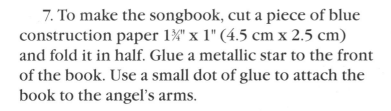

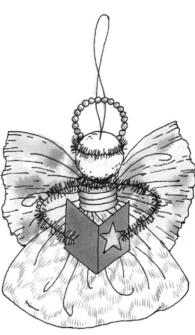

7. To make the songbook, cut a piece of blue construction paper 1¾" x 1" (4.5 cm x 2.5 cm) and fold it in half. Glue a metallic star to the front of the book. Use a small dot of glue to attach the book to the angel's arms.

13

SUPER SNOWMAN

You will need:

- ★ 4" x 8" (10 cm x 20 cm) piece of lightweight cardboard
- ★ pencil
- ★ tracing paper
- ★ scissors
- ★ polyfill or cotton
- ★ glue or glue stick
- ★ tissue paper or face tissue
- ★ *½ silver tinsel pipe cleaner*
- ★ white thread
- ★ black marker
- ★ scrap of red construction paper
- ★ 4" x 8" (10 cm x 20 cm) piece of white bond or construction paper
- ★ *4" (10 cm) length of purple paper twist*
- ★ *10" (25 cm) length of jumbo yarn or bright-colored ribbon*
- ★ ornament hook (optional)

This snowman is guaranteed not to melt. Make a bunch of them and decorate your tree, the door to your room, or holiday gift packages.

1. Transfer the snowman pattern onto the cardboard. (See page 1.) Make two snowman shapes on the cardboard. Cut them out.

2. Place a small amount of polyfill in the middle of each section of the cardboard snowman shape. Use two or three small dots of glue to attach each section of polyfill to the cardboard.

3. Place the snowman shape polyfill-side down on top of the tissue. Wrap the tissue around the cardboard and polyfill. Glue the tissue to the back of the cardboard. Carefully cut the extra tissue away.

SNOWMAN PATTERN

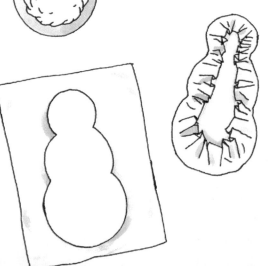

4. Repeat steps 2 and 3 with the second cardboard snowman. Place both snowman shapes back to back.

5. Cut off ½" (1.5 cm) of the tinsel pipe cleaner and set it aside. To make the snowman's arms, curl the remaining length of pipe cleaner and place it between the two snowman shapes. Glue the two halves of the snowman together with the pipe cleaner between them. Let the glue dry.

6. Wrap white thread around the snowman's waist 4 times. Knot the ends together. Put a tiny drop of glue on the knot.

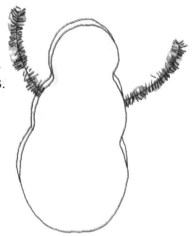

7. Wrap white thread around the snowman's neck 4 times. Knot the ends together and glue the knot.

8. Cut the ½" (1.5 cm) piece of piper cleaner in half to make eyebrows. Glue them to the snowman's face. Use just a little glue and be careful not to drip the glue on the tissue.

9. With a black marker, make two dots for eyes. Cut a small rectangle out of the red construction paper for the mouth. Carefully glue the mouth in place using a small amount of glue.

TOP HAT

1. Transfer the hat brim and crown patterns onto white bond or construction paper. (See page 1.) Cut the shapes out.

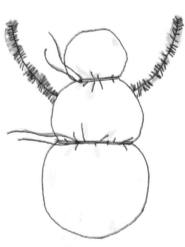

2. Unwind and flatten the 4" (10 cm) paper twist. Glue the paper to the hat brim and crown and let it dry. Carefully cut away the paper that hangs over the edges. Cut another piece to fit on the underside of the brim. Save it and all the scraps.

BRIM PATTERN

CROWN PATTERN

3. Roll the hat crown into a tube. Hold it together and slide the tube inside the central circle of the brim. Keeping the crown rolled in a tube, pull it away from the brim. Glue the crown together so that it stays in the shape of a tube.

4. Push the crown through the brim so that ⅛" (.3 cm) of the crown sticks out below the brim. Make little snips with the scissors in the part of the crown below the brim. Fold back the tabs you have just made. Glue them to the brim. Glue the paper you already cut for the underside of the brim over the tabs.

FINAL TOUCHES

1. Glue the hat to the snowman's head.

2. To make the buttons, cut two small circles out of the paper twist scraps. With a tiny dot of glue, attach the buttons to the front of the snowman.

3. Tie jumbo yarn around your snowman's neck, and attach an ornament hook to the back. Now your snowman is ready to sparkle on your Christmas tree!